Lillenas®

MW00414256

All THE BEST FOR PIANO AND ORGAN

A Treasury of Classic Duet Arrangements

14 Arrangements by

Bill FASIG, John INNES, James PETHEL, Stan PETHEL, Linda SPRUNGER, Ron SPRUNGER, Herman VOSS, Eleanor WHITSETT

Lillenas® PUBLISHING COMPANY

KANSAS CITY, MO 64141

www.lillenas.com

CONTENTS

4

A Mighty Fortress Is Our God

Sw. Full
Gt.   Full - no Reeds
Ped. 16', 8'

MARTIN LUTHER
Arranged by John Innes and Bill Fasig

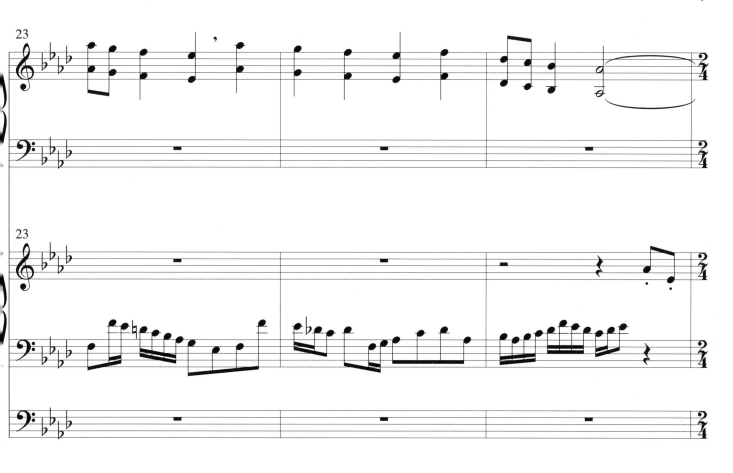

8

Savior, Like a Shepherd Lead Us

(with excerpts from *CLAIR DE LUNE* - Claude Debussy)

Sw.   Warm Solo stop
Gt.   Soft Flutes and Strings 8'
Ped. Lieblich Ged. 16'

WILLIAM B. BRADBURY
Arranged by Ron and Linda Sprunger

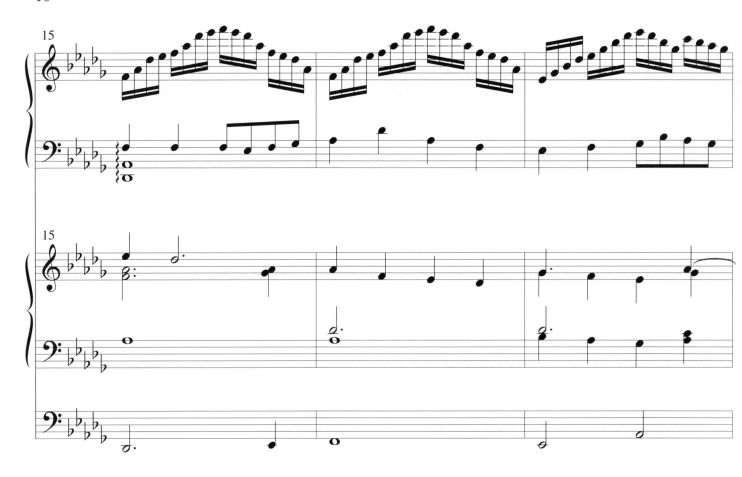

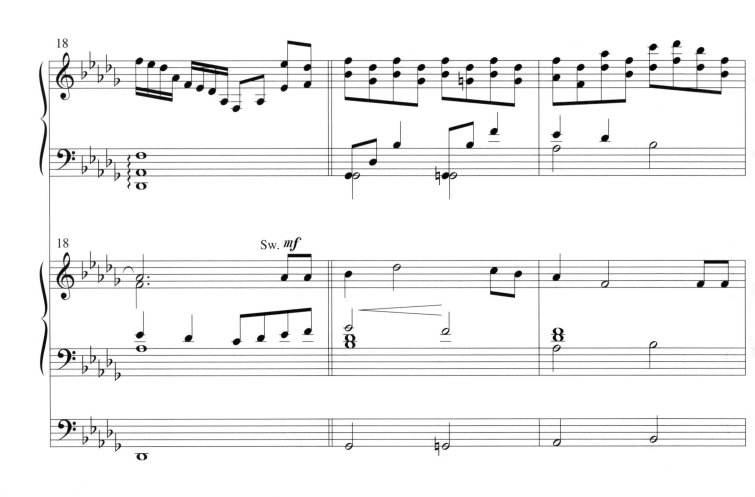

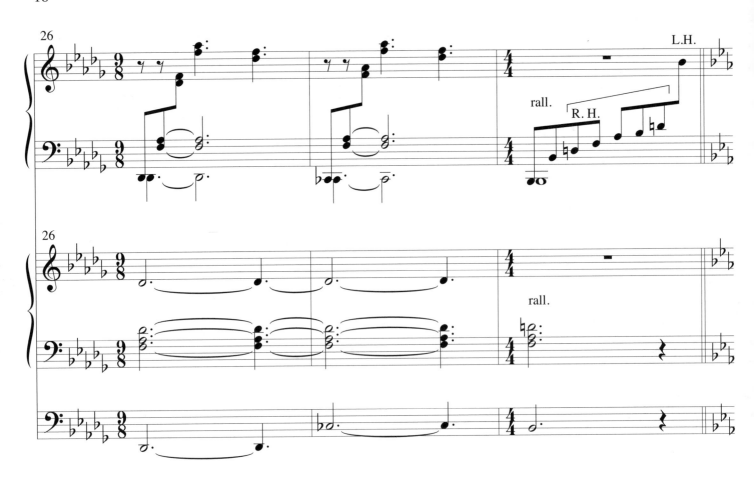

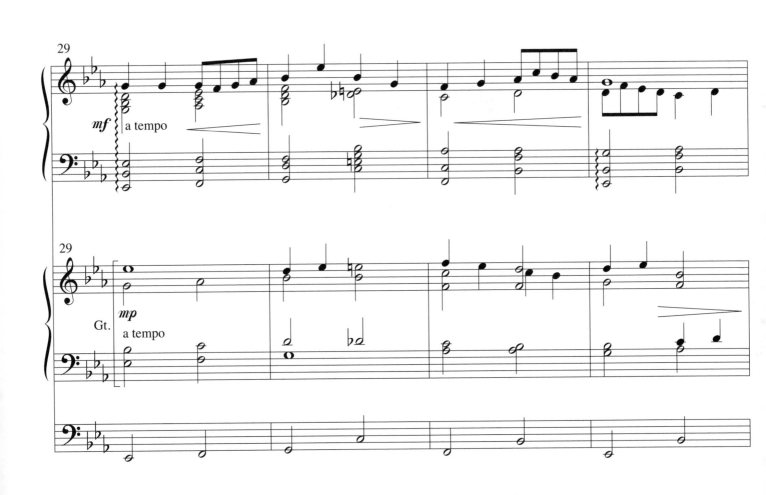

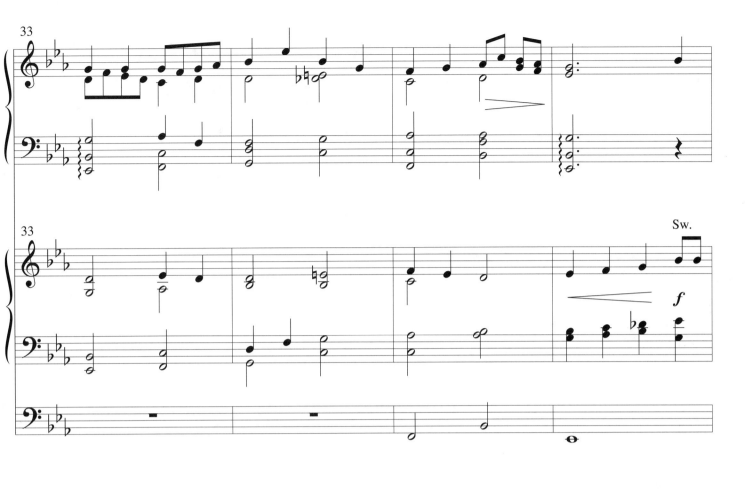

Praise Ye the Lord, the Almighty

Sw.   Oboe 8'
Gt.   Principals 8', 4', 2²/₃', 2'
Ped. Principals 16', 8'

from *Stralsund Gesangbuch*
Arranged by John Innes and Bill Fasig

Moderately fast

24

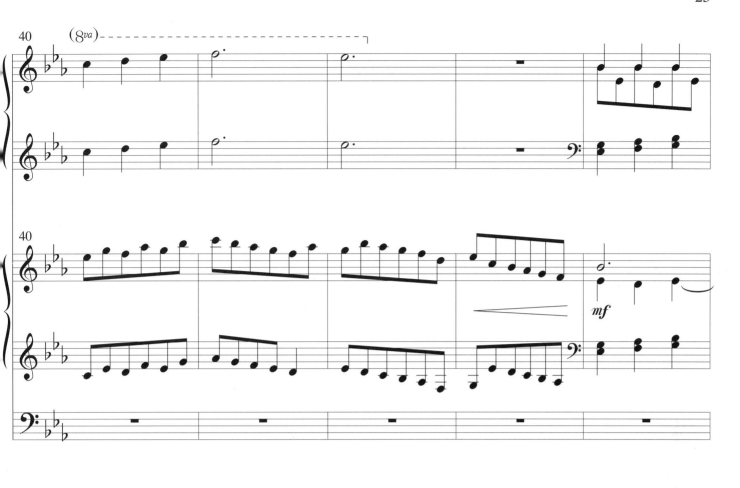

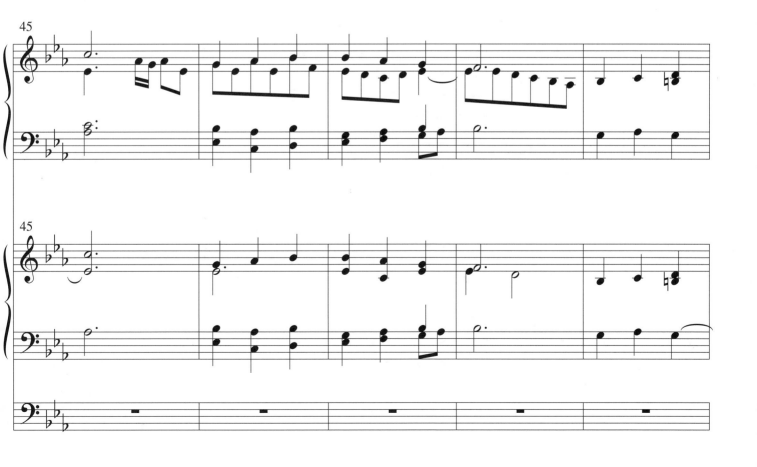

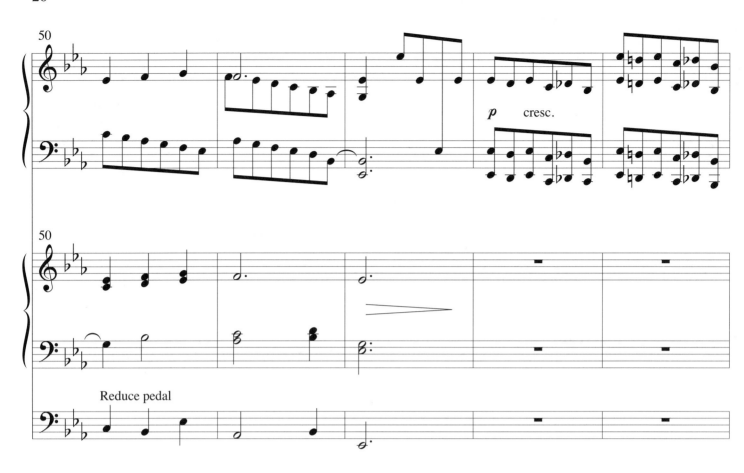

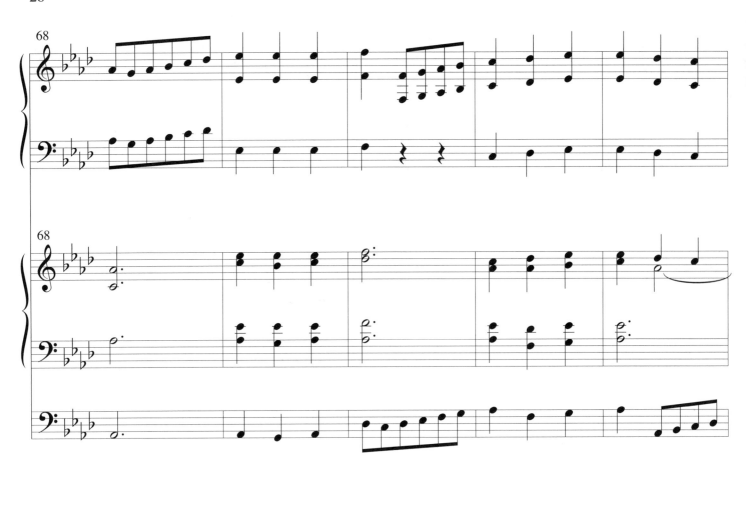

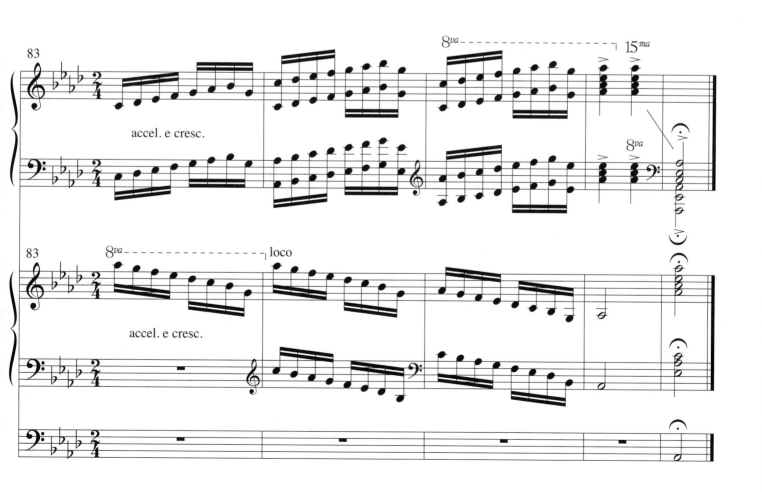

Blessed Assurance

Sw. Soft Flute, Strings
Gt. Solo Flute
Ped. Bourdon 16', Bass Flute 8'

PHOEBE PALMER KNAPP
Arranged by Eleanor Whitsett

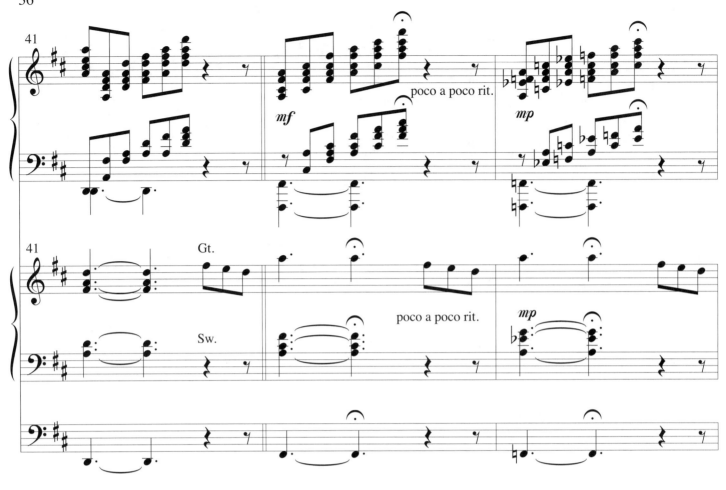

Come, Thou Almighty King

Sw.   Diapason 8', Reeds 8', 4'
Gt.   Flutes 8', 2'
Ped. 16', 8'

FELICE de GIARDINI
Arranged by James Pethel and Stan Pethel

38

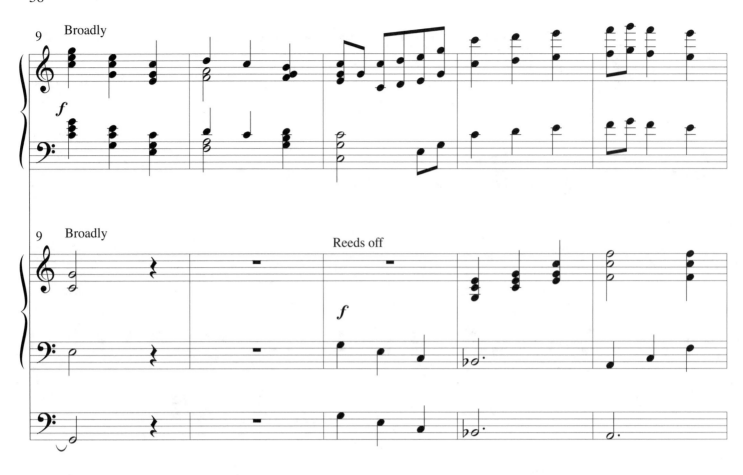

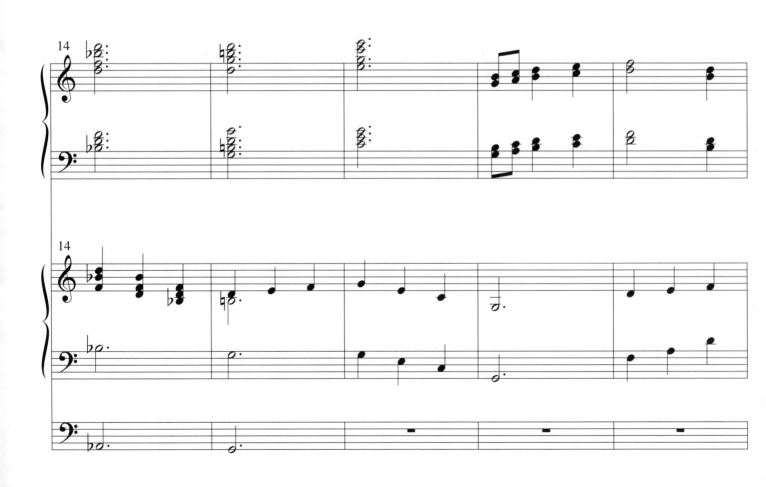

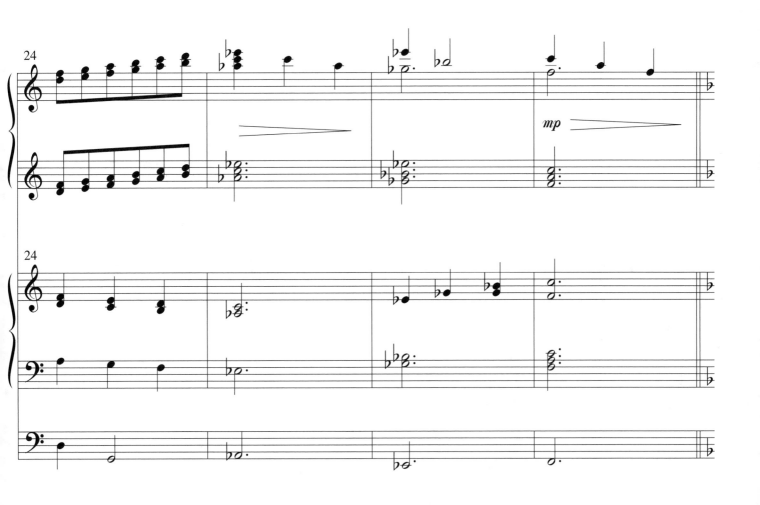

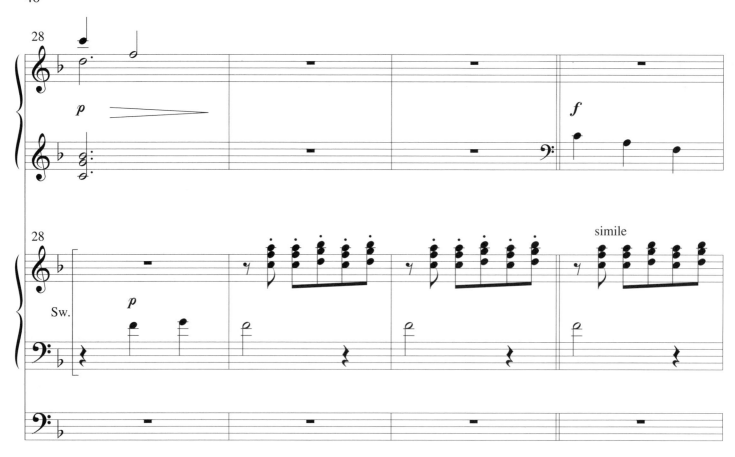

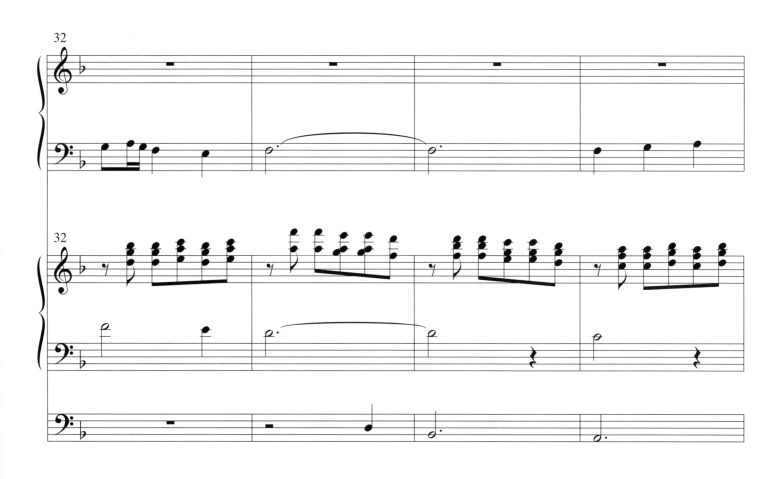

46

Glorious Things of Thee Are Spoken

Sw. Trumpet, Diapason 8', 4'
Gt. Diapason 8', 4', 2'
Ped. 16', 8'

FRANZ JOSEPH HAYDN
Arranged by John Innes and Bill Fasig

Fairly brisk tempo

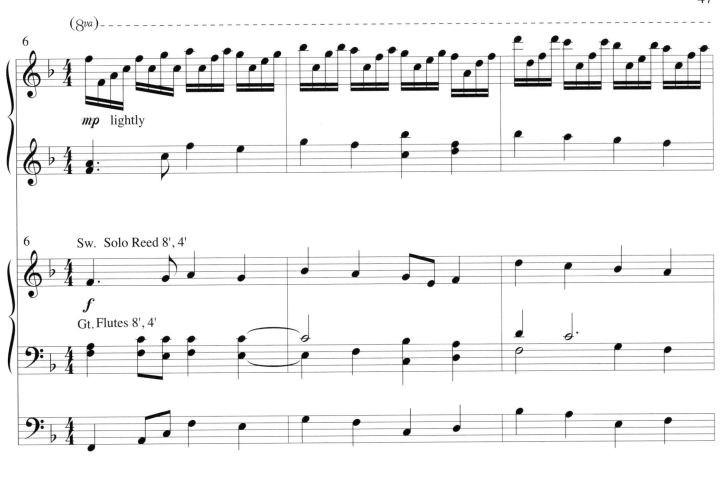

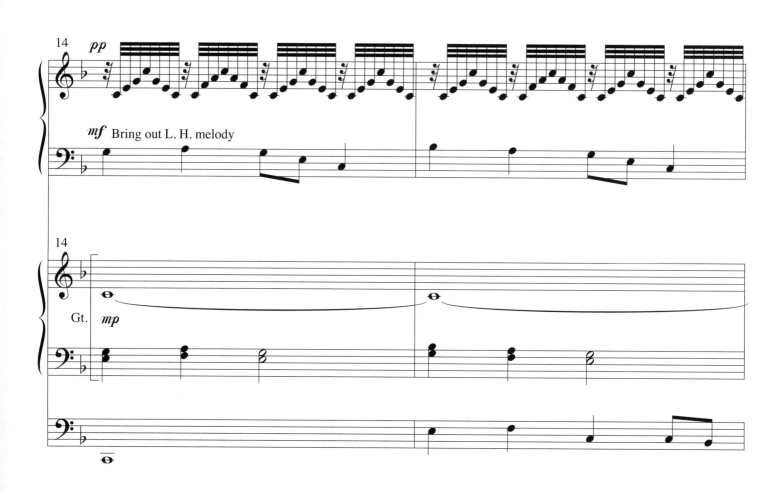

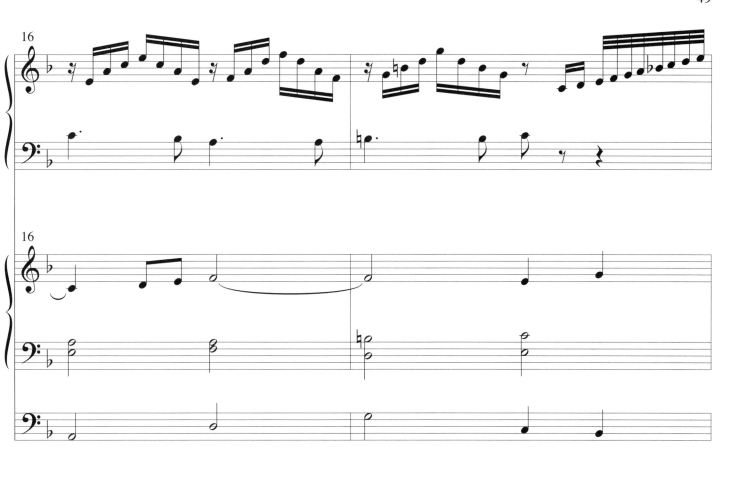

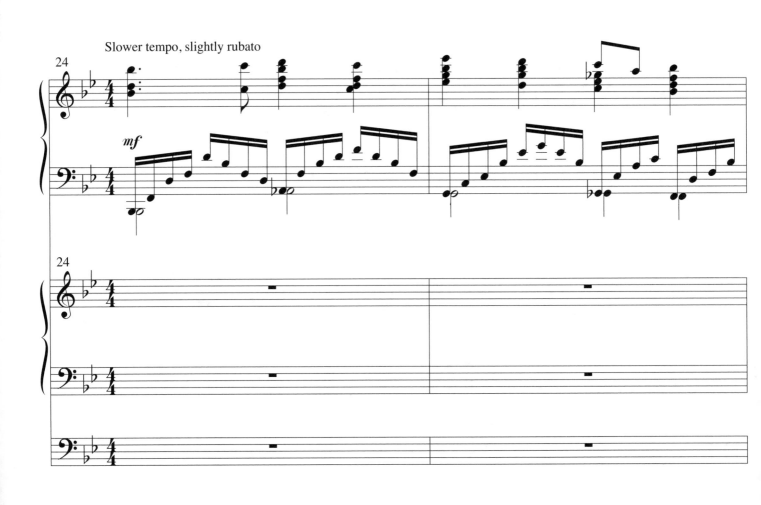

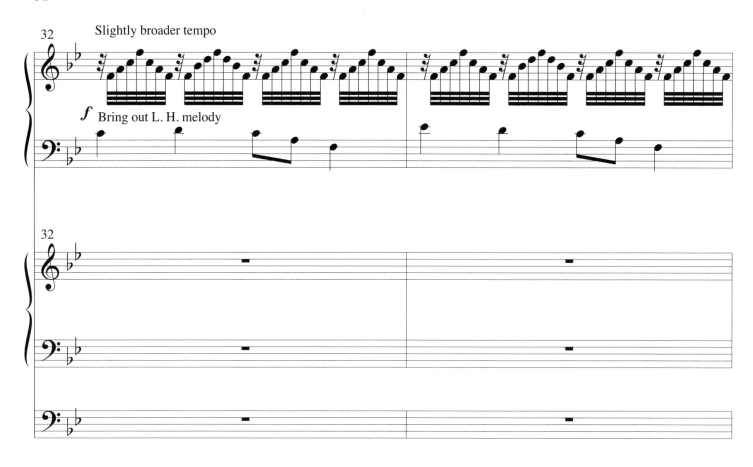

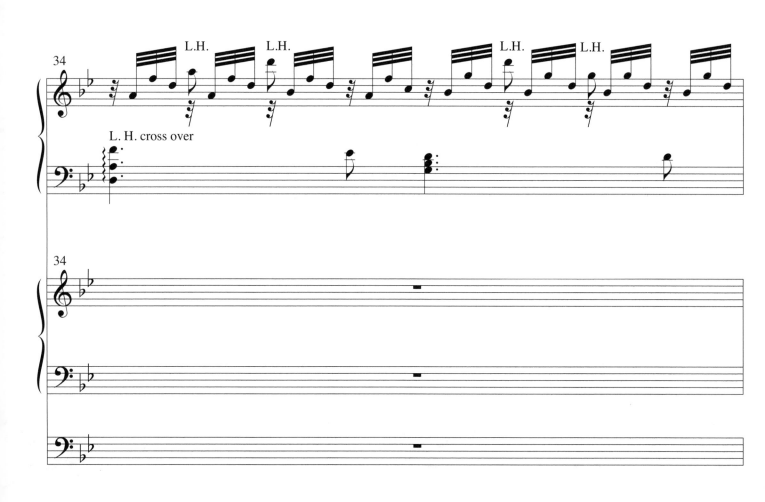

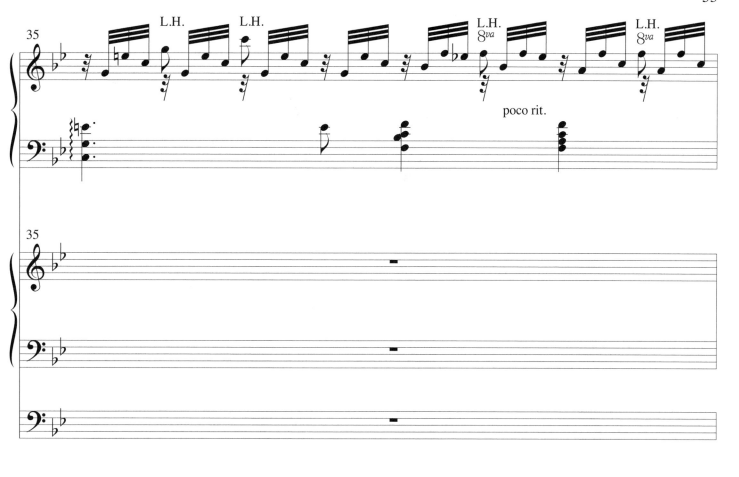

God So Loved the World

Sw. Solo Flute 8'
Gt. Strings, Flutes 8', 4'
Ped. 16', 8'
With feeling

JOHN STAINER
Arranged by Eleanor Whitsett

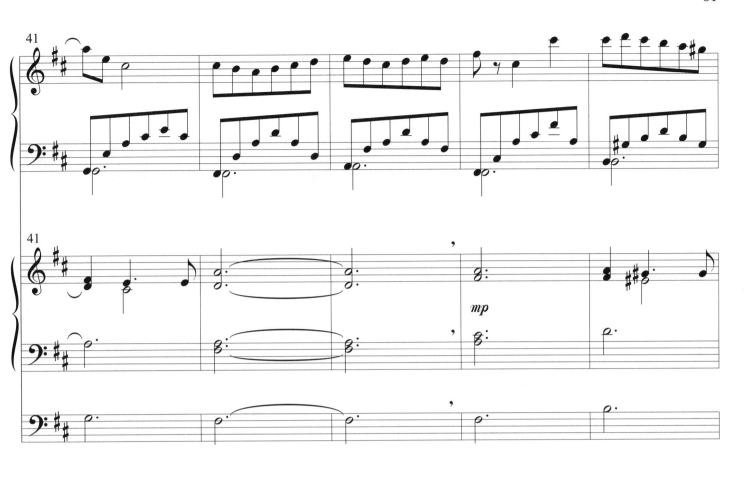

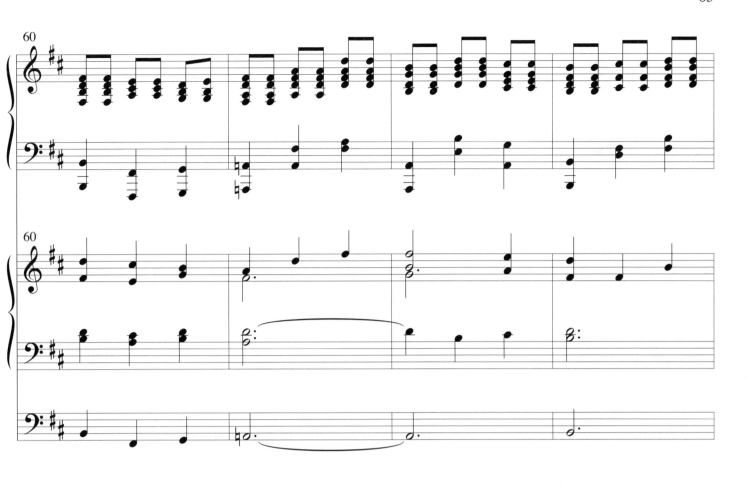

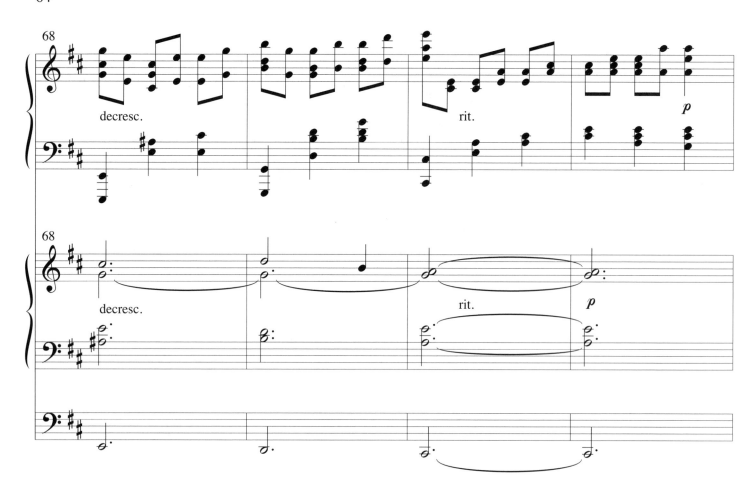

66

His Eye Is on the Sparrow

Sw.   Geigen diapason 8', Flutes 8', 4'
Gt.   Soft solo stop
Ped. Flutes 16', 8', 4'
      Rubato, in a relaxed style

CHARLES H. GABRIEL
Arranged by Ron and Linda Sprunger

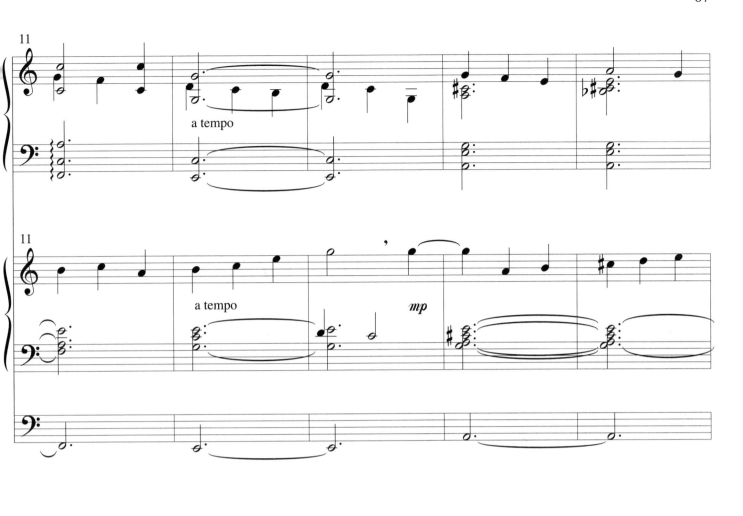

68

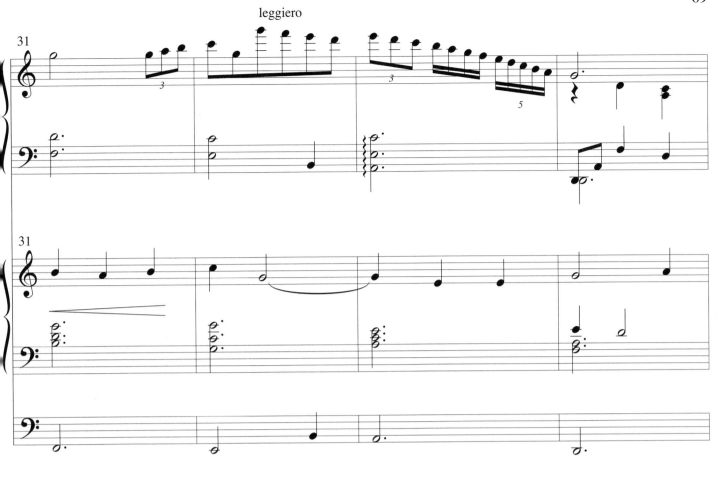

70

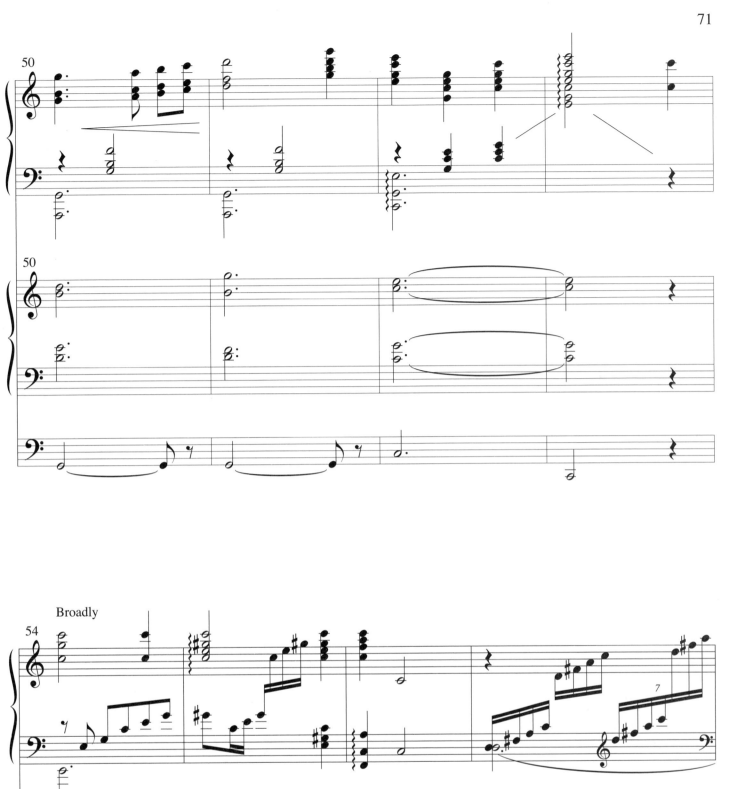

Broadly

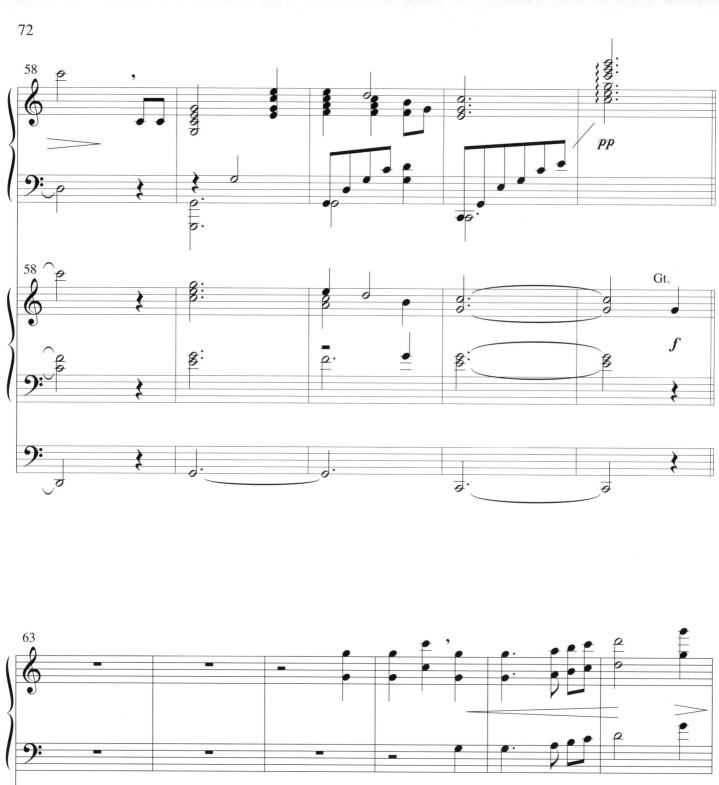

Jesu - Noel

Sw. Oboe 8'
Gt. Stopped Diapason 8'
Ped. Gedect 16', Light 8'
Moderato

Jesu, Joy of Man's Desiring
JOHANN SEBASTIAN BACH
The First Noel
from W. Sandy's *Christmas Carols*
Arranged by Eleanor Whitsett

Jesus Is All the World to Me

Sw.   Flutes 8', 4'; Principals 8'
Gt.   Principals 8', 4', 2'
Ped. 16', 8'

WILL L. THOMPSON
Arranged by James Pethel and Stan Pethel

84

America, the Beautiful

Sw. Solo Reed 8'
Gt. Principals 8', 4', 2'
Ped. Principals 16', 8'

SAMUEL A. WARD
Arranged by John Innes and Bill Fasig

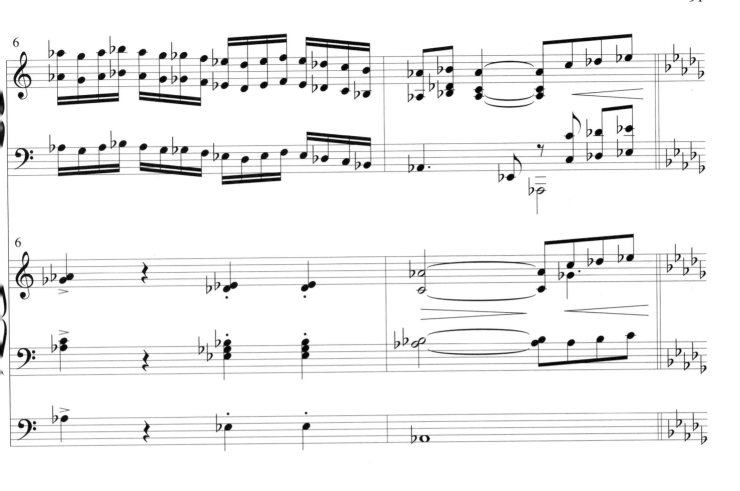

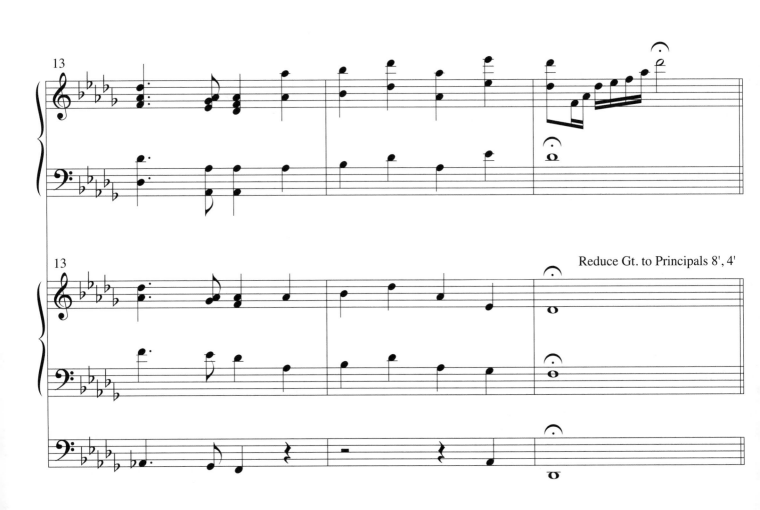

Reduce Gt. to Principals 8', 4'

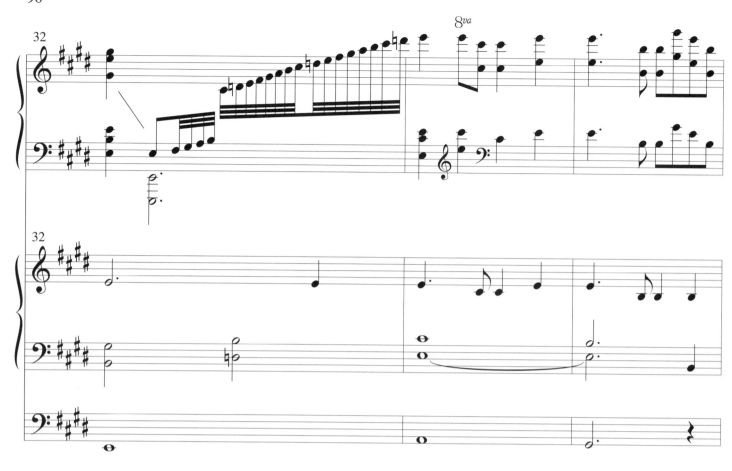

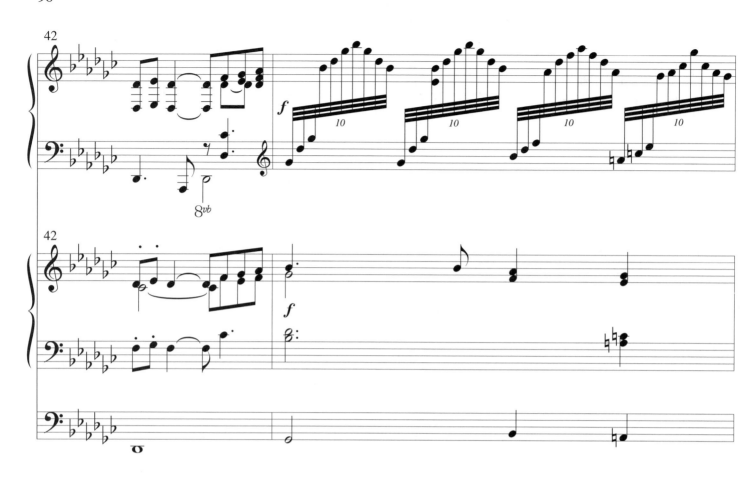

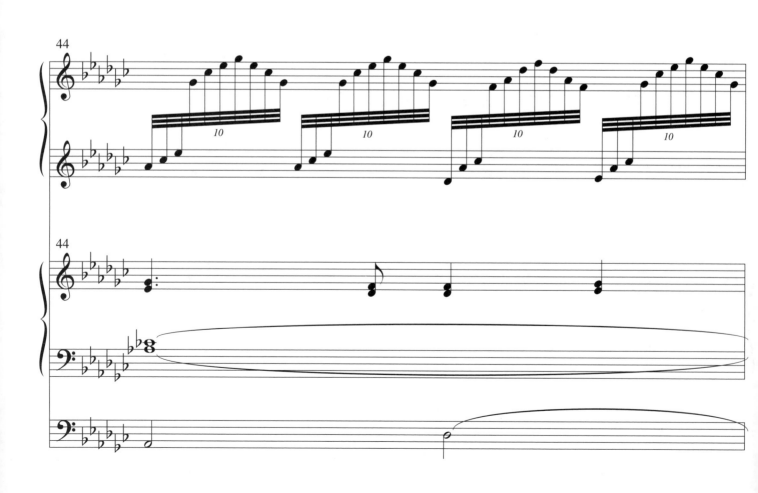

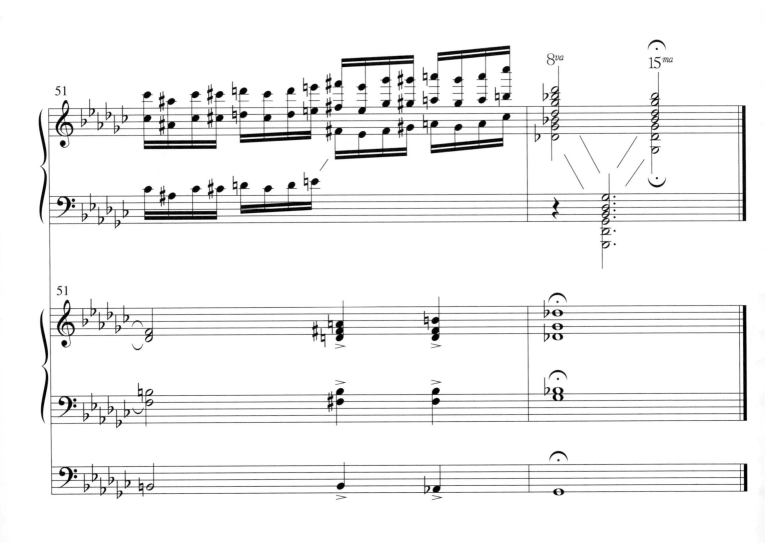

All Creatures of Our God and King

Sw. Flutes 8', 4', 2' or Principals 8', 4'
Gt.   Full; Gt. to Gt. 4'
Ped. 16', 8'

from *Geistliche Kirchengesang*
Arranged by John Innes and Bill Fasig

Brisk tempo

(no sustaining pedal, but legato)

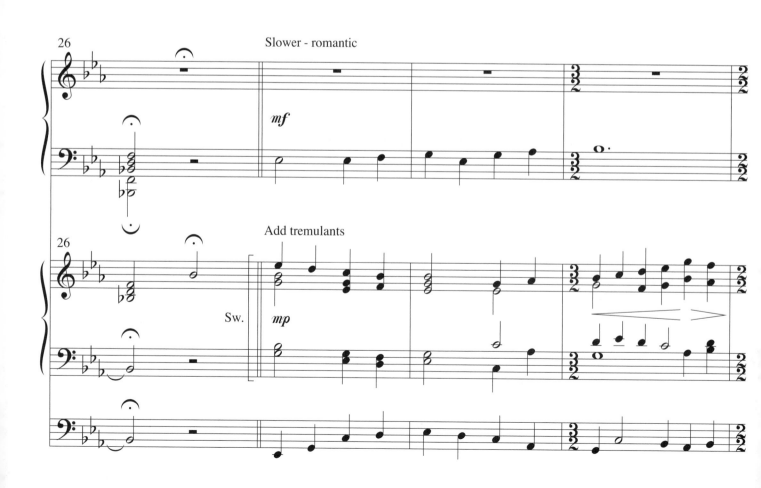

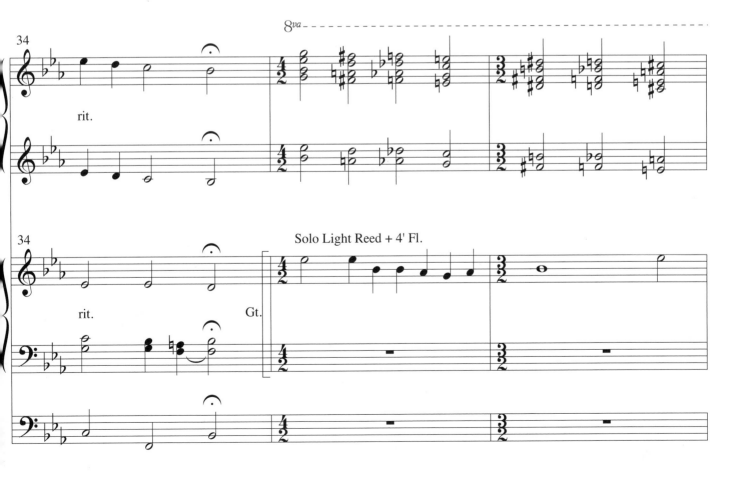

Rejoice, Ye Pure in Heart

Sw. Full without Reeds
Gt. Principals; Trem. off
Ped. 16' Sw. to Ped.

ARTHUR H. MESSITER
Arranged by Herman Voss

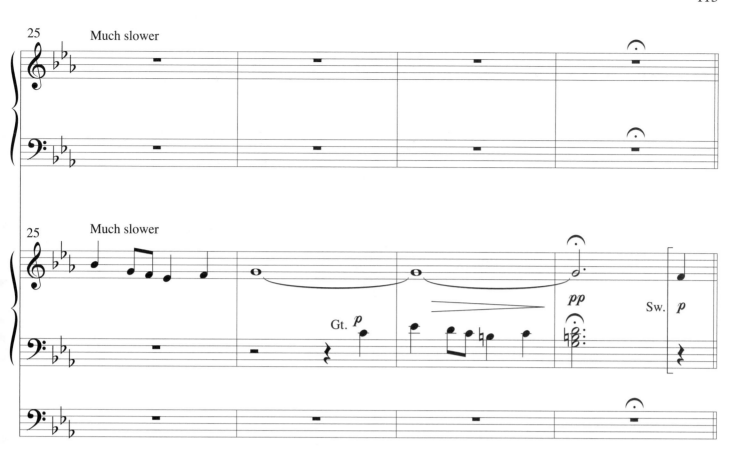

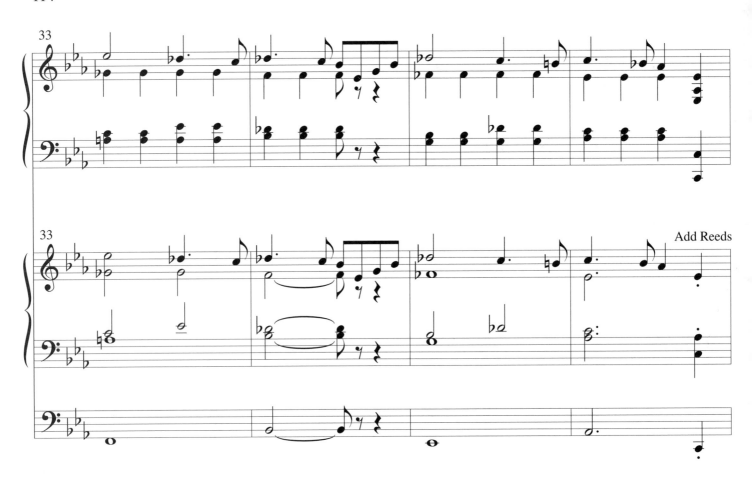

Add Reeds

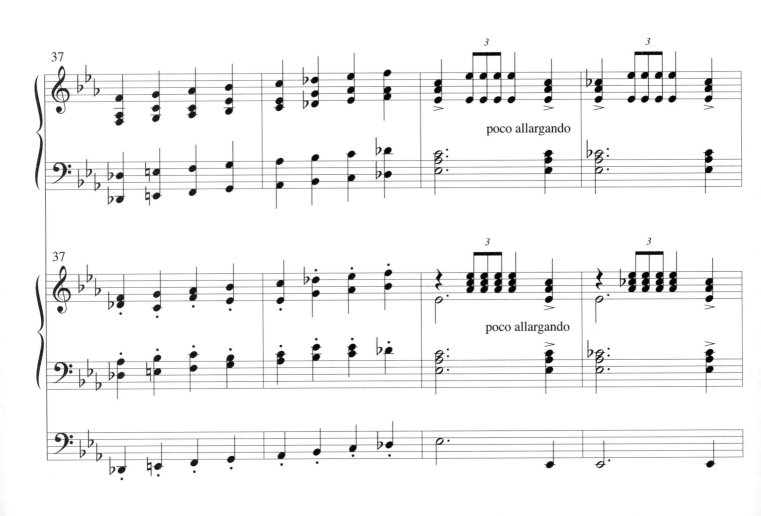

poco allargando

poco allargando

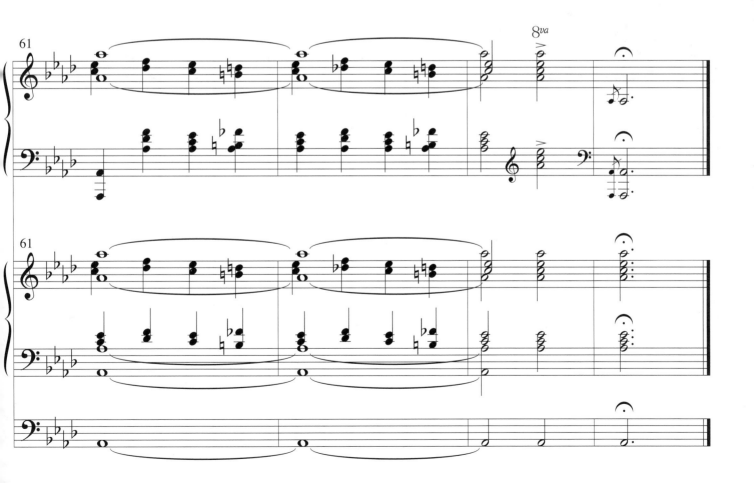

When Morning Gilds the Skies

Sw.   Oboe 8', Flute 4'
Gt.   Flutes 8', 4'
Ped. Bourdon 16', 8'

JOSEPH BARNBY
Arranged by John Innes and Bill Fasig

Softly, as from a distance

Sw. prepare: Oboe, Flute off.
Add Principals 8', 4'
String Celeste with trem.

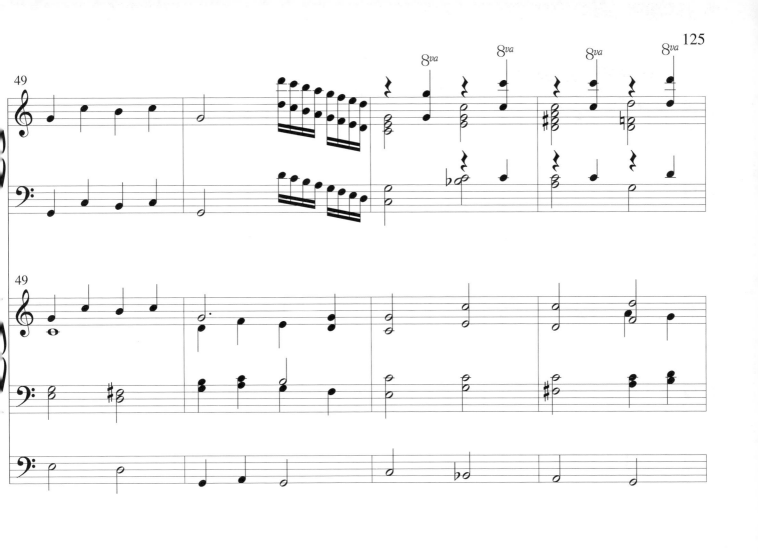

As before

pp legato

Sw. Strings off. Add Oboe 8', Flute 4'
Gt. Prepare Soft Flutes 8', 4'

As before

Sw. *p*

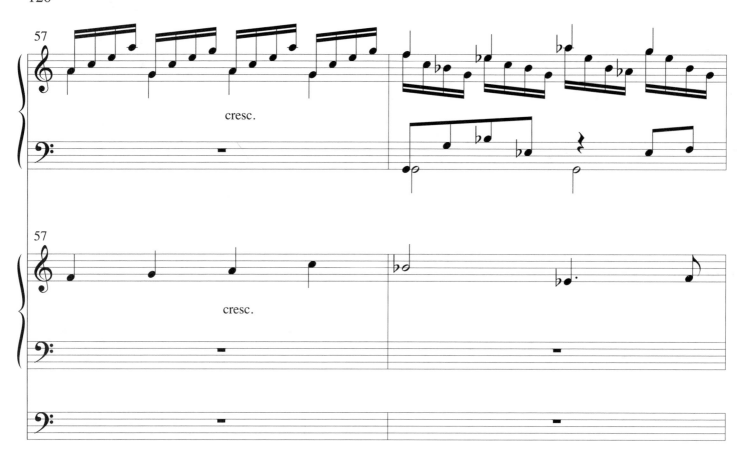

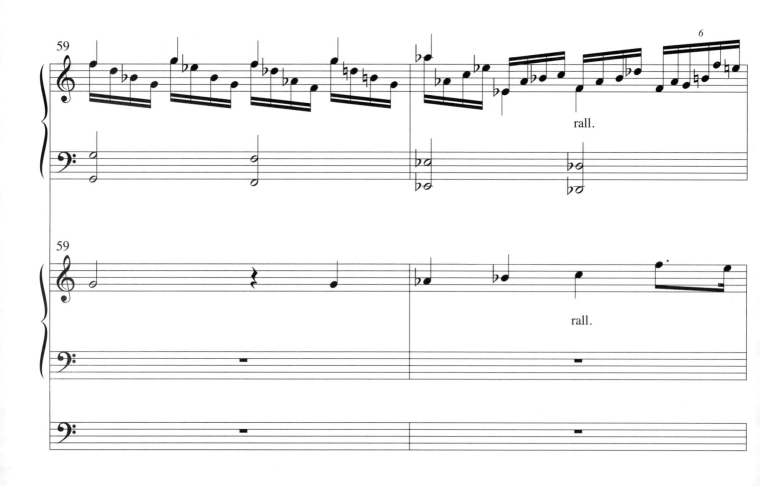